PRIMARY SOURCES OF
FAMOUS PEOPLE IN AMERICAN HISTORY™

BENJAMIN FRANKLIN

EARLY AMERICAN GENIUS
POLÍTICO E INVENTOR ESTADOUNIDENSE

MAYA GLASS

TRADUCCIÓN AL ESPAÑOL:
TOMÁS GONZÁLEZ

rosen central
Primary Source™

Editorial Buenas Letras™

The Rosen Publishing Group, Inc., New York

Published in 2004 by The Rosen Publishing Group, Inc.
29 East 21st Street, New York, NY 10010

First Bilingual Edition 2004
First English Edition 2004

Cataloging Data

Glass, Maya.
Benjamin Franklin : early American genius / by Maya Glass.
    v. cm. — (Primary sources of famous people in American history)
Contents: Benjamin Franklin the apprentice — A struggle and a success — Printer
and citizen — Benjamin Franklin the inventor — Benjamin Franklin, great American.
ISBN 0-8239-4151-5 (lib. bdg.)
1. Franklin, Benjamin, 1706–1790—Juvenile literature. 2. Statesmen—United States—
Biography—Juvenile literature. 3. Inventors—United States—Biography—Juvenile
literature. 4. Printers—United States—Biography—Juvenile literature. 5. Scientists—
United States—Biography—Juvenile literature. [1. Franklin, Benjamin, 1706–1790.
2. Statesmen. 3. Scientists. 4. Inventors. 5. Printers. 6. Spanish Language Materials—
Bilingual
I. Title. II. Series: Primary sources of famous people in American History (New York, N.Y.)
E302.6.F8 G55 2003
973.3'092—dc21

Manufactured in the United States of America

Photo Credits: cover © Francis G. Mayer/Corbis; p. 5 © National Portrait Gallery, Smithsonian Institution/Art
Resource, NY; p. 7 Dover Pictorial Archive Series; p. 11 The American Philosophical Society; pp. 13, 17, 27, 29
Library of Congress Prints and Photographs Division; pp. 15, 25 © Hulton /Archive/Getty Images; p. 19 Cigna
Museum and Art Collection; p. 21 Franklin Institute; p. 23 Archives Charmet/The Bridgeman Art Library

CONTENTS

CONTENIDO

1 BENJAMIN FRANKLIN THE APPRENTICE

Benjamin Franklin was born on January 17, 1706, in Boston, Massachusetts. Benjamin was the fifteenth of seventeen children. When he was eight, he went to school. He did not stay long in school because his family needed him to work. Benjamin became an apprentice to his father at age ten.

---

1 BENJAMÍN FRANKLIN, APRENDIZ

Benjamín Franklin nació el 17 de enero de 1706 en Boston, Massachusetts. Benjamín fue el decimoquinto de diecisiete hijos. Entró a la escuela a la edad de ocho años, pero no asistió durante mucho tiempo, pues su familia necesitaba que trabajara. Benjamín se hizo aprendiz de su padre a los diez años de edad.

Benjamin Franklin never stopped learning. He always read books and used his mind.

Benjamín Franklin nunca dejó de aprender. Siempre leía libros y ejercitaba la mente.

Benjamin learned how to make soap and candles. Benjamin did not like the work. He liked reading better. He then became an apprentice to his brother James. They worked as printers. Printers are people who make newspapers and books for people to read.

————◆◆◆————

Benjamín aprendió a fabricar jabón y velas, pero no le gustaba ese trabajo. Prefería leer. Entonces se hizo aprendiz en el taller de su hermano James, que era impresor. Los impresores hacen periódicos y libros para que la gente lea.

Printing in colonial times took skill and was learned over many years.

Imprimir en la época colonial exigía habilidad y muchos años para aprender el oficio.

James Franklin started his own newspaper in 1721. Benjamin wanted to write for the paper. James thought his brother was too young to write well. Benjamin wrote articles using a different name, Mrs. Silence Dogood. The articles made fun of the Puritans in Boston. Sometimes Benjamin took over the printing.

James Franklin fundó su propio periódico en 1721. Benjamín quería escribir para el periódico, pero James pensaba que su hermano era demasiado pequeño y no sabría hacerlo bien. Benjamín escribió artículos bajo el nombre de "Señora Silence Dogood". En ellos se burlaba de los puritanos de Boston. A veces él mismo se encargaba de imprimirlo.

THE New-England Courant.

[N° 37]

From MONDAY April 9. to MONDAY April 16. 1722.

Ben Franklin was only sixteen when he began to write essays in the *New-England Courant*.

Franklin tenía apenas dieciséis años cuando empezó a escribir ensayos para el periódico *New-England Courant*.

9

2 A STRUGGLE AND A SUCCESS

Benjamin Franklin moved to New York in 1723. He was seventeen years old. He did not find work there. A printer told him to try Philadelphia. In Philadelphia, Franklin worked with the printer Samuel Keimer. During this time, Franklin met Deborah Read. She would later become his wife. Franklin wanted to start his own printing shop.

---

2 LUCHA Y ÉXITO

En 1723, cuando tenía diecisiete años, Benjamín Franklin se mudó a Nueva York. Pero no encontró empleo allí. Un impresor le aconsejó que buscara trabajo en Filadelfia. En esa ciudad, Franklin trabajó con el impresor Samuel Keimer. En ese tiempo conoció a Deborah Read, quien más tarde sería su esposa. Franklin quería fundar su propia imprenta.

Deborah Read saw quickly that Franklin was smart and witty.

Deborah Read rápidamente se dio cuenta de que Franklin era inteligente e ingenioso.

Franklin had no money to start his own shop. He sailed to London to try getting loans. He needed equipment. He did not have much luck. He went to work as a teacher. In 1726, he went back to Philadelphia to work again with Samuel Keimer. In 1728, Franklin opened a printing shop with Hugh Meredith.

———◆◆◆———

Franklin no tenía dinero para fundar su propio taller. Viajó a Londres a fin de tratar de conseguir préstamos para comprar el equipo. No tuvo mucha suerte. Empezó a trabajar de maestro y en 1726 regresó a Filadelfia donde volvió a trabajar con Samuel Keimer. En 1728, Franklin abrió un taller de imprenta en compañía con Hugh Meredith.

Ben Franklin used this printing press in his Philadelphia print shop.

Franklin usó esta máquina impresora en su taller de Filadelfia.

3 PRINTER AND CITIZEN

In 1729, Benjamin Franklin bought Samuel Keimer's newspaper, the *Pennsylvania Gazette*. People loved to read Franklin's lively writing. The paper sold well in Philadelphia. In 1730, Franklin and Deborah Read were married by common law. Common law meant they had lived together long enough to be considered married.

---

3 IMPRESOR Y CIUDADANO

En 1729, Benjamín Franklin compró el periódico Pennsylvania Gazette, propiedad de Samuel Keimer. Al público le encantaba la manera vivaz como escribía Franklin, y el periódico se vendió bien en Filadelfia. En 1730, Franklin y Deborah Read se casaron por derecho consuetudinario. Esto significaba que habían vivido bastante tiempo juntos y por consiguiente se los declaraba casados.

THE
Pennſylvania GAZETTE.

Numb. XL.

Containing the freſheſt Advices Foreign and Domeſtick.

From Thurſday, September 25. to Thurſday, October 2. 1729.

THE Pennsylvania Gazette *being now to be carry'd on by other Hands, the Reader may expeĉt ſome Account of the Method we deſign to proceed in.*

Upon a View of Chambers's great Dictionaries, from whence were taken the Materials of the Universal Instructor in all Arts and Sciences, which uſually made the Firſt Part of this Paper, we find that beſides their containing many Things abſtruſe or inſignificant to us, it will probably be fifty Years before the Whole can be gone thro' in this Manner of Publication. There are likewiſe in thoſe Books continual References from Things under one Letter of the Alphabet to thoſe under another, which relate to the ſame Subject, and are neceſſary to explain and compleat it; theſe taken in their Turn may perhaps be Ten Years diſtant; and ſince it is likely that they who deſire to acquaint themſelves with any particular Art or Science, would gladly have the whole before them in a much leſs Time, we believe our Readers will not think ſuch a Method of communicating Knowledge to be a proper One.

However, tho' we do not intend to continue the Publication of thoſe Dictionaries in a regular Alphabetical Method, as has hitherto been done; yet as ſeveral Things exhibited from them in the Courſe of theſe Papers, have been entertaining to ſuch of the Curious, who never had and cannot have the Advantage of good Libraries; and as there are many Things ſtill behind, which being in this Manner made generally known, may perhaps become of conſiderable Uſe, by giving ſuch Hints to the excellent natural Genius's of our Country, as may contribute either to the Improvement of our preſent Manufactures, or towards the Invention of new Ones; we propoſe from Time to Time to communicate ſuch particu-

There are many who have long deſired to ſee a good News-Paper in Pennsylvania; and we hope thoſe Gentlemen who are able, will contribute towards the making This ſuch. We ask Aſſiſtance, becauſe we are fully ſenſible, that to publiſh a good News-Paper is not ſo eaſy an Undertaking as many People imagine it to be. The Author of a Gazette (in the Opinion of the Learned) ſhould be qualified with an extenſive Acquaintance with Languages, a great Eaſineſs and Command of Writing and Relating Things cleanly and intelligibly, and in few Words; he ſhould be able to ſpeak of War both by Land and Sea; be well acquainted with Geography, with the Hiſtory of the Time, with the ſeveral Intereſts of Princes and States, the Secrets of Courts, and the Manners and Cuſtoms of all Nations. Men thus accompliſh'd are very rare in this remote Part of the World; and it would be well if the Writer of theſe Papers could make up among his Friends what is wanting in himſelf.

Upon the Whole, we may aſſure the Publick, that as far as the Encouragement we meet with will enable us, no Care and Pains ſhall be omitted, that may make the Pennsylvania Gazette as agreeable and uſeful an Entertainment as the Nature of the Thing will allow.

The Following is the laſt Meſſage ſent by his Excellency Governour *Burnet,* to the House of Repreſentatives in *Boſton.*

Gentlemen of the Houſe of Repreſentatives,

IT is not with ſo vain a Hope as to convince you, that I take the Trouble to anſwer your Meſſages, but, if poſſible, to open the Eyes of the deluded People whom you repreſent, and whom you are at ſo much Pains to keep in Ignorance of the true State of their Affairs. I need no

The *Pennsylvania Gazette* came out once each week. The newspaper was just a few pages long.

El *Pennsylvania Gazette* salía una vez por semana. El periódico tenía pocas páginas.

Benjamin Franklin's *Poor Richard's Almanack* came out in 1732. An almanac is a book that has recipes and information such as weather reports. Farmers use it to help them know when to plant their crops. The printing shop went so well that Franklin hired help. He wanted to spend more time on science and politics.

En 1732 se publicó el *Poor Richard's Almanack*, de Benjamín Franklin. Los almanaques son libros que traen recetas e información variada, por ejemplo sobre el clima. Los granjeros los utilizan para saber cuándo plantar sus cosechas. La imprenta iba tan bien que Franklin contrató más personal. Deseaba dedicar más tiempo a la ciencia y la política.

Note, This ALMANACK us'd to contain but 24 Pages, and now has 36; yet the Price is very little advanc'd.

Poor RICHARD improved:

BEING AN

ALMANACK

AND

EPHEMERIS

OF THE

MOTIONS of the SUN and MOON;

THE TRUE

PLACES and ASPECTS of the PLANETS;

THE

RISING and *SETTING* of the *SUN*;

AND THE

Rifing, Setting *and* Southing *of the* Moon,

FOR THE

BISSEXTILE YEAR, 1748.

Containing alfo,

The Lunations, Conjunctions, Eclipfes, Judgment of the Weather, Rifing and Setting of the Planets, Length of Days and Nights, Fairs, Courts, Roads, &c. Together with ufeful Tables, chronological Obfervations, and entertaining Remarks.

Fitted to the Latitude of Forty Degrees, and a Meridian of near five Hours Weft from *London*; but may, without fenfible Error, ferve all the NORTHERN COLONIES.

By *RICHARD SAUNDERS*, Philom.

PHILADELPHIA:

Franklin wrote *Poor Richard's Almanack* as a fun way to help people live a good life.

Escribir el *Poor Richard's Almanack* era una manera divertida de ayudar a la gente a vivir bien.

Franklin helped Philadelphia in many ways. Around 1740, he invented a stove that was better than the ones used at the time. He held meetings so people could talk about their ideas. He served as deputy postmaster of the colonies from 1753 to 1774. He also helped to form a fire-fighting company, a police force, and a library in Philadelphia.

⸺◆◆◆⸺

Franklin ayudó a la ciudad de Filadelfia de muchas maneras. Hacia 1740, inventó una estufa mejor que las que se utilizaban en esa época. Franklin convocaba reuniones para que la gente diera a conocer sus ideas. Entre 1753 y 1774 trabajó como administrador adjunto de los correos de las colonias. También ayudó a crear un cuerpo de bomberos, un departamento de policía y una biblioteca para la ciudad.

Ben Franklin helped form fire and police departments in Philadelphia.

Franklin ayudó a formar los departamentos de bomberos y de policía en Filadelfia.

4 BENJAMIN FRANKLIN THE INVENTOR

Ben Franklin invented many things. He invented a stove to heat a house. He also made bifocal glasses. Bifocals are special glasses that help people see both near and far. He invented lightning rods, too. These metal rods are put on houses to protect them.

---

4 BENJAMÍN FRANKLIN, EL INVENTOR

Franklin inventó muchas cosas, como un tipo de estufa para calentar las casas y los lentes bifocales. Éstos son lentes especiales que permiten a la gente ver de cerca y también de lejos. Franklin además inventó el pararrayos, que es un tubo de metal que se pone en las casas para protegerlas en las tormentas.

In the 1740s, Franklin invented an iron furnace stove. It needed less wood to heat a larger area.

En la década de 1740, Franklin inventó una estufa de hierro que necesitaba menos leña y calentaba un espacio mayor.

Franklin wanted to prove that lightning was a form of electricity. It is thought that he did a lightning experiment in 1752. He flew a kite with a metal key on it. The key got hit by lightning and was filled with electricity. The electricity went from the kite to Franklin, and he felt a shock. That is how Franklin knew that lightning was electric.

———◆◆◆———

Franklin quería demostrar que los rayos eran una forma de electricidad. Se cree que en 1752 hizo un experimento haciendo volar una cometa con una llave sujeta a ella. La llave recibió la descarga de un rayo y quedó electrizada. La electricidad bajó de la cometa hasta Franklin, quien sintió una descarga. Así fue como supo que los rayos eran electricidad.

CHOCOLAT POULAIN
GOÛTEZ ET COMPAREZ — QUALITÉ SANS RIVALE

FRANKLIN.

Ben Franklin had an idea that lightning was a form of electricity. He tested his theory and found out that he was right.

Franklin tenía la idea de que los rayos eran una forma de electricidad. Probó su teoría y encontró que tenía razón.

5 BENJAMIN FRANKLIN, GREAT AMERICAN

Benjamin Franklin became a politician. He worked in London to get the British to listen to the colonies. Britain ruled the colonies during the 1700s. The colonies wanted to rule themselves. Events in America led to the American Revolution. The Stamp Act placed a tax on many printed items. The act made the colonies angry.

---

5 BENJAMÍN FRANKLIN, EL GRAN ESTADOUNIDENSE

Benjamín Franklin se convirtió en político. Trabajó en Londres para lograr que los británicos escucharan a las colonias. Durante la década de 1700, los británicos gobernaban a las colonias, pero éstas querían gobernarse a sí mismas. Los acontecimientos en Norteamérica llevaron a la Guerra de Independencia. La ley conocida como Acta de Sellos gravó con impuestos muchos materiales impresos. Esta ley enojó a los colonos.

American colonists in the 1770s no longer wanted to pay British taxes. This drawing shows British tax collectors fleeing from angry colonists.

Ya en la década de 1770 los colonos norteamericanos se rehusaban a pagar impuestos a los británicos. En este dibujo aparecen recaudadores de impuestos británicos huyendo de colonos enojados.

The Boston Massacre happened on March 5, 1770. British soldiers shot a group of colonists who did not have guns. This made colonists hate the British even more. In 1773, Britain taxed tea. Colonists dressed as Native Americans dumped boxes of tea into Boston Harbor. This was known as the Boston Tea Party.

La Matanza de Boston se produjo el 5 de marzo de 1770. Los soldados británicos dispararon sobre un grupo de colonos desarmados. Esto hizo que los colonos se enojaran aún más. En 1773, los británicos gravaron el té con impuestos. Colonos vestidos como indios norteamericanos lanzaron cajas de té a la bahía de Boston. A esto se lo llamó la Fiesta del Té de Boston *(Boston Tea Party)*.

The anger that built up during the 1770s caused the Boston Massacre. British troops killed five colonists during the fighting.

La indignación que se acumuló durante la década de 1770 llevó a que se produjera la Matanza de Boston. En esa revuelta las tropas británicas mataron a cinco colonos.

In 1775, Franklin returned to Philadelphia. He became a member of the Continental Congress. Thomas Jefferson wrote the Declaration of Independence in 1776. Franklin was one of the people to sign it. Benjamin Franklin worked to serve his country for the rest of his life. He died on April 17, 1790.

———◆◆◆———

En 1775, Franklin regresó a Filadelfia y se hizo miembro del Congreso Continental. Thomas Jefferson escribió la Declaración de Independencia en 1776. Franklin fue una de las personas que la firmó. Benjamín Franklin trabajó sirviendo al país durante el resto de su vida. Murió el 17 de abril de 1790.

Ben Franklin was a wise old man by the time Thomas Jefferson wrote the Declaration of Independence.

Cuando Thomas Jefferson escribió la Declaración de Independencia, Benjamín Franklin era ya un anciano sabio.

TIMELINE

1706—Benjamin Franklin is born on January 17.

1718—Franklin becomes a printer's helper to his brother James.

1730—Franklin and Deborah Read are married.

1765—Franklin and others protest the Stamp Act.

1776—Franklin reads and signs the Declaration of Independence.

1790— Franklin dies on April 17 in Philadelphia. He is 84 years old.

CRONOLOGÍA

1706—Benjamín Franklin nace el 17 de enero.

1718—Franklin se hace ayudante de su hermano James, que es impresor.

1730—Franklin y Deborah Read se casan.

1765—Franklin y otros protestan contra el Acta de Sellos.

1776—Franklin firma la Declaración de Independencia.

1790—Franklin muere el 17 de abril en Filadelfia a los 84 años de edad.

GLOSSARY

apprentice (uh-PREN-tis) A person who learns a trade by working for an experienced person.

colonies (KOL-uh-neez) A territory settled by people from another country and controlled by that country.

common-law marriage (KAH-mun-LAW MAR-ij) A marriage between a man and a woman who have lived together for a certain period of time.

politician (pah-lih-TIH-shun) A person who holds or runs for a public office.

politics (PAH-lih-tiks) The science of government and elections.

Puritans (PYUR-ih-tenz) Members of a religious group in England who moved to America during the seventeenth century.

WEB SITES

Due to the changing nature of Internet links, the Rosen Publishing Group, Inc., has developed an online list of Web sites related to the subject of this book. This site is updated regularly. Please use this link to access the list:

http://www.rosenlinks.com/fpah/bfra

GLOSARIO

aprendiz (el, la) Persona que aprende un oficio trabajando con alguien experimentado.

colonia (la) Territorio en el que se establece gente de otro país y es gobernado por dicho país.

matrimonio por derecho consuetudinario Matrimonio entre un hombre y una mujer que han vivido juntos durante cierto tiempo.

política (la) Ciencia del gobierno y las elecciones.

político(-ca) Persona que desempeña un cargo público o aspira a desempeñarlo.

puritanos(-as) Miembros de un grupo religioso de Inglaterra que se estableció en Norteamérica durante el siglo XVII.

SITIOS WEB

Debido a las constantes modificaciones en los sitios de Internet, Rosen Publishing Group, Inc. ha desarrollado un listado de sitios Web relacionados con el tema de este libro. Este sitio se actualiza con regularidad. Por favor, usa este enlace para acceder a la lista:

http://www.rosenlinks.com/fpah/bfra

INDEX

ABOUT THE AUTHOR

Maya Glass is a writer and editor living in New York City.

ÍNDICE

ACERCA DEL AUTOR

Maya Glass es escritora y editora. Vive en la ciudad de Nueva York.